4

Copyright 2007 by Sally Moffet
Salt Grass Press
P.O. Box 291
Fulton, Texas 78382
Orders: www.SaltGrassPress.com

Illustrations by C. Blum
Photographs by Capt. Sally Moffett

First printing 2007
United States of America
ISBN 978-0-9793980-2-5

Saltwater
Kayak Fishing the Texas Way

A Beginner's Handbook

Captain Sally Ann Moffett

Dedication

I dedicate this book to my father,
Art Dulski, who gave to me my love and respect
for the outdoors and an absolute passion for fishing.
His love, trust and encouragement led me to believe that there
was nothing that I could not achieve or become.

Everything You Need to Know to Get Started with Texas Saltwater Kayak Fishing
By Captain Sally A. Moffett

Introduction ■ Kayak Fishing & Me 1

Chapter 1 ■ Choosing the Right Kayak 7

Chapter 2 ■ Rigging Your Fishing Kayak.................... 15

Chapter 3 ■ What to Take and How to Take It 23

Chapter 4 ■ What to Wear... 27

Chapter 5 ■ Getting Your Kayak to the Water........ 34

Chapter 6 ■ Paddling Your Kayak.............................. 38

Chapter 7 ■ Weather, Safety and Communication 40

Chapter 8 ■ When Things Go Wrong 46

Chapter 9 ■ Now You're Ready to Fish! 56

Conclusion 71

Kayak & Tackle Checklists 72

Books can't make you a good fisherman,
but they can make you a better one.

Old Fisherman's Saying

Introduction

Kayak Fishing and Me

From the time I was a little girl living on the waters of Lake Erie with my dad, mom and little sister, I have always had a passion for fishing. My entire life has been spent on the water, with the past 25 years fishing the saltwater bays of South Texas.

My father always wanted a son, but got stuck with me. Hunting and fishing were his passion and I was his partner on every trip. Dragging a too-big game coat filled with pheasant, watching our hunting dogs chase rabbits or helping drive our Chris Craft cabin cruiser to favorite pickerel fishing places wasn't a typical little girl life. My dad even made me a "special" pair of waders by cutting arm holes in the top of the chest of a big pair of men's waders, letting me have freedom of movement as I fetched ducks and decoys in the icy water of the Great Lakes. My Mom, Dad, sister Kim and I spent summers like Indians in the Upper Peninsula of Michigan, Canada, Minnesota and Wisconsin, fishing all of the secret lakes and streams and watching wildlife. In the winter, we drove our camper south, pulling a boat to Florida where we fished, swam and oystered in the warm waters near West Palm Beach. It was about 16 years into my partnership with my dad when he finally realized that I was, indeed,

Some of the best times of my life were spent with my family in the outdoors.

1

a **girl**. Panic stricken, he announced to all of the boys in our small hometown that I was off-limits under penalty of death. So much for a social life!

My father passed away from cancer between my junior and senior year of high school, and with him passed the idyllic life-style that I had come to take for granted. I missed him. This loss became a defining moment of my life.

When I graduated from high school in 1978 I left behind a college scholarship, my small hometown and my many memories. I decided my new home was going to be Oz ... Houston, Texas. With $300, a car, a 9 month old black lab named Butch, a TV and a stereo, the trip from Erie, Michigan to Houston, Texas was indeed a grand adventure. I had always wanted a horse, and, of course, everyone in Texas had horses ... but just as important, I needed to be close to the water. Houston could provide all of that, plus a job! Checking into a hotel room, I looked over the want ads, made a phone call and got an interview the same afternoon. The Art Institute of Houston was looking for an admissions secretary. Typing wasn't my best skill since I had been mostly a jock in high school and jocks didn't generally take typing class. But, as luck would have it, the job was mine at the fine starting salary of $650 a month. I found an apartment for $250 all bills paid which left me lots of money to spare.

I quickly became aware of the advantages ... and fun of kayak fishing.

I had arrived! Houston was booming, and success and horses came my way and I felt the future was bright. In late 1984, however, a carjacking and a brush with death told me that Houston might not be the place for me.

My mom had since moved to Rockport to help her sister operate a small hotel there and so I visited every weekend. The friendly people and the relaxed life-style along the coast reminded me of how important nature was to me. Viewing my life in Houston as similar to wading bootless with stingrays, I decided that Rockport might be a better life choice. With my horses, dogs and cats we eagerly made the journey to my new life on the coast. My destiny, it seems, was to find my way back to the kind of life that my dad had enjoyed and passed on to me. It took about five years to get there, but sometimes felt a lot longer.

Being a new, full-time resident of Rockport, the first thing I bought when I got into town was a new fishing boat. Legendary guide and friend Capt. James Fox helped pick a brand new 16' Fishin' Ski Barge with a 40 hp Johnson motor, complete with a cavitation plate for a quicker hole shot (even though I was not completely sure what a "hole shot" was!) The new boat was totally different from what I had known up north. It was rigged out for shallow water fishing, complete with a poling platform, carpet and a VHF radio. It was definitely the best "chick boat" on the coast. Actually, I think it must have been the only "chick boat" on the coast at the time since I got a lot of looks and comments at the boat ramp. Things like "for a blonde, you can sure back up a boat trailer!" and "does your husband know you have his boat?" I guess South Texas just wasn't quite ready for a 24 year old female boat captain in 1984!

Though I had a "real" job back then, I fished every single moment I could. My boss at the time, a veteran lawyer seeking his own peace and quiet, kept a small office overlooking the water in Rockport. He owned several boats and was an avid fisherman as well. He understood about "perfect" fishing days ... Paralegal work could generally be put off till the wind blew and the rain started.

After several years, I took a chance and embarked on a new adventure. I was offered a great job working for the CEO of one of the largest biotech companies in Southern California. San Diego became my new address, but it was a far cry from the life I had enjoyed in Rockport. I missed my boat. I missed my horses. It was a high pressure environment with no decent fishing within a two-hour drive. I not only felt very much like a fish out of water, I was beginning to feel like a cooked fish. Money isn't everything. I got back to Rockport and Texas just as soon as I could.

In 1994, Rockport was again home sweet home. I resumed my paralegal career and was lucky to find work with one of the most respected attorneys in Texas ... and a devout fly fisherman. He totally understood when I told him I couldn't hold down a real job because it would interfere with my fishing. He hired me as a contract paralegal with my own office in downtown Corpus Christi. I worked when things needed to get done and I fished all of the other times. After almost 5 years working some great cases with my boss, I reluctantly informed him that it was time for me to change careers. When I told him I was going to become a full time fishing guide, his only comment was "it's about time!".

Most guides at the time used natural baits since that's what the clients were used to. I decided that I needed a new boat, one with bait wells and lots of fishing room and found a 24' Carolina Skiff. It was lightly used, priced just right and looked like it could hold a bunch of people. That skiff was a workhorse. With it I caught lots of fish and I really learned the bays.

After completing the 100 ton Master's Captain's License course, and using sea time that had accumulated throughout my life, I qualified for my USCG 25-ton near-coastal Master's Captain's License.

With my new boat, a Master's Captain's License and an enthusiastic vision of my future, Captain Sally's Reel Fun Charters was born. I was only the second woman fishing guide on the coast at that time. New fishermen and families with children were my core business and bait fishing for redfish with excited kids turned out to be a real blast. I always tried to share with those folks some of the same excitement and respect for nature that my father had shared with me.

Surviving my first year as a rookie fishing guide, I went to the Shallow Water Fishing Expo in Houston. It was there that I listened and watched as Capt. Chuck Scates showed what fly fishing for redfish in the shallow water was all about. I was hooked, and I decided right there that my next goal was to somehow get Capt. Chuck to teach me the fine points of fly casting. After a few months of being annoying and persistent, he decided to meet in a parking lot at Cove Harbor in Rockport for my first lesson. What a disaster! But it wasn't long before my technique had improved to the point that Chuck finally agreed to take me fishing.

I remember that first fly fishing expedition like yesterday. Chuck parked his custom boat on a shoreline and we watched a flock of seagulls diving down into a small shallow lake near Hog Island Hole. While Chuck grabbed his camera, I tentatively grabbed my fly rod and we walked toward the activity. The water was being thrashed by several large groups of redfish feeding on shrimp in this small, muddy lake. In my excitement, I managed to forget everything that I learned in the parking lot and even though it was only 30 feet to the fish, casting my fly to these hungry redfish seemed impossible. Frustration took over and I failed to cast even close to one of these redfish. Chuck got some unbelievable close-up photos of fish chasing shrimp and I gained a new respect for the sport I was pursuing. It was a lot harder than it looked, and even more so when the fisherman is paralyzed with buck fever!

Eventually, Chuck took me fly fishing again. Catching that first redfish on the fly was unforgettable. We were poling around a point in the Lighthouse Lakes on a sunny, bright day in water only 6" deep and crystal clear as vodka. I spotted a big redfish cruising alone, following the grass shoreline with his back slightly out of the water. I was ready this time, and holding my excitement in check, the fly actually made it somewhere in the vicinity of my redfish's face. I suddenly and explosively had a fish on! This was the moment I had worked for the past six months. After landing this spectacular fish, Chuck offered me a fisherman's handshake and took the photo of my first red on the fly. Looking at that picture today still brings back memories ... and a smile. Now I remember and share that moment every time a client catches their first redfish on the fly.

Once "spoiled" by fly fishing, bait fishing held absolutely no interest for me. My dilemma was simple. I was an absolute nobody

My First Red on a fly!

PHOTO by CAPT. CHUCK SCATES

surrounded by the likes of Capt. Chuck Scates and Capt. Chuck Naiser, the Godfathers of coastal fly fishing and I wasn't even sure if there was a place for me in shallow water fishing. In addition, being a new fishing guide I had to take care of my customers with the boat I already owned. There was absolutely no way that I could afford one of those fancy poling skiffs that fly fishing guides used.

One of my friends who peruses garage sales showed up one day with a used Ocean Kayak complete with seat and paddle. He had purchased it for almost nothing, but sort of wondered what it was good for. We both stood there and looked it over ... a kayak is not an imposing sight. He left it in my yard to pick up later. So I put it in my Carolina Skiff and took it fishing with me.

I remembered I had been seeing fish in a small lake in Talley Island. There was always lots of bait blowing up and plenty of bird action, but I had never been able to reach it ... Too shallow by boat and much too soft for wading. So I parked my big boat on the shoreline and along with my new fly rod and a few flies, easily paddled through a slough. As I silently entered the clear shallows I saw a group of coppery-red tails showing just off a point of grass. This was the cartoon light-bulb moment ... So THIS was what kayaks were for! After that day, nothing else mattered but the vision of tailing redfish off the bow. Kayak fly fishing became my new passion. It seems that I had my work cut out for me.

Venturing into uncharted waters, where no fishing guide had gone before was a leap of faith on my part. Other fishing guides thought I was crazy. They were convinced that no one would want to paddle their own boats, sight cast or even fly fish. But I knew I was on to something and so I pressed ahead.

Taking my message on the road, I talked about the merits of kayak fishing everywhere I went. Pretty soon, a few of my clients called and wanted to give this new style of fishing a try! This opened a few eyes. They had a great time, told some friends, and more clients came. Within a year, there was a wave of excitement building for kayak fishing on the Texas Coast.

Clearly, being a trailblazer is a risky maneuver. In this case, however, it paid off incredibly! Kayak fishing, fly fishing and shallow water sightcasting is now the hottest sport on the Texas Coast - I am proud to be the first one to bring it to you!

This book should help you enjoy the sport of kayak fishing on the Texas Coast more fully. Hopefully the information you gather here will help jump-start you from beginner to seasoned angler in no time!

Chapter 1

Choosing the Right Kayak
for YOU ...

Perhaps the toughest choice a new kayak fisherman will make will be which kayak to purchase. Even if you listen to all of your kayak fishing friends advice, visit internet kayak fishing chat sites and try to absorb everything that you read, it's **still** difficult to wade through the details and find that "perfect" kayak. This chapter will try to explain what each and every feature can do for you so that you can put together a chart to help you decide how to narrow down the choices. Use the chart at the end of the chapter and take it to your favorite kayak retailer. Let them help you find a kayak that suits your fishing style, body type and budget.

What follows on the next few pages are some basic points to consider in your decision to purchase a fishing kayak.

Your local kayak shop can be a valuable resource both for gear and accessories as well as first hand knowledge and experience.

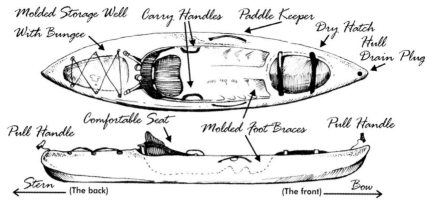

Molded Storage Well With Bungee   *Carry Handles*   *Paddle Keeper*   *Dry Hatch*   *Hull Drain Plug*

Pull Handle   *Comfortable Seat*   *Molded Foot Braces*   *Pull Handle*

Stern (The back)   (The front) *Bow*

A Typical Sit on Top Kayak

Kayak Length

Kayaks today are available in lengths from 8 feet to 18 feet. They are designed from very narrow to very wide, light, heavy, with seats built in, sit inside, sit on top, with pedals, with a rudder and without. It's a tough choice, but if you know what your individual needs and style are, the decision can be narrowed down. In a fishing kayak, length equals speed. If you need to cover long distances to get to your fishing grounds, you may want to consider a long kayak, which is 14 feet in length or more. One consideration in purchasing a longer kayak might be how you would be hauling it and loading it, or if it will fit on the top of your vehicle. We'll address the mechanics of that issue in another chapter, but take into consideration your abilities ... it might be difficult to lift a longer, heavier kayak onto the roof of your vehicle without help if you are a person who is not very tall or strong.

Kayak Width

Kayak width equals kayak stability. The wider your kayak, the more it will resist rolling from side to side. . . BUT, wide kayaks are not as quick over the water. If you want to go fast, don't buy a wide kayak. Kayaks with widths above 29 inches would be considered in the most stable range. If you would like to stand up on

8

your kayak to drift or cast, for the ultimate in stability look at a kayak that is at least 30 inches wide or more.

Basic Rule:

Length = Speed

Width = Stability

Kayak Weight

Modern kayaks typically weigh between 45 pounds and 75 pounds. Don't buy a kayak you can't lift, load or move around single-handedly. If you aren't able to manage your kayak by yourself, you probably won't get as much use out of it. The whole point of kayak fishing after all is to be self-contained and self-sufficient.

Sit on Top Kayaks

A sit on top kayak is typically styled like a comfortable platform. As the name implies, the paddler sits right on top, and not enclosed within the boat. This style of kayak makes for a relatively easy and quiet entry and exit when using your kayak for wade fishing. Obviously, sit on top kayaks are most popular in warmer environments.

Sit Inside Kayaks

A sit inside kayak offers the paddler the opportunity to sit down inside the kayak's "cockpit", an enclosed area that can be "skirted" to keep the paddler completely dry. These kayaks are typically round-bottomed in design and in general, not as stable as a sit-on-top kayak. A sit inside kayak is particularly preferred by paddlers in cold water environments or when touring long distances. Designed for easy and smooth gliding, the kayak allows the paddler to cover long distances with less energy. Due to the popularity of kayak fishing, there is a trend toward manufacturers to offer sit inside kayaks with enhanced stability making them worth a good look when picking your kayak.

Pedal Powered Kayaks

Several manufacturers have designed ingenious pedaling systems for kayaks that allow for quicker propulsion. These kayaks need more room below the water for the mechanics and perform best in lake, river or bay environments where the angler is fishing in a foot of water or more. Pedaled kayaks allow for "hands-free" kayaking and permit the angler to move his kayak without the use of a paddle while fishing and casting.

Rudder Systems

One of the most often debated accessories are kayak rudder systems. After reading all of the chatter back and forth on the kayak fishing boards it's still a tough decision whether to invest the additional money into a rudder installation or not ... They are one of the more expensive equipment additions. Deciding on a rudder system will always be based on some basic issues.

Because of the ease of turning and steering, a rudder can sometimes extend the time a novice paddler can spend on the water by allowing them to use their energy most efficiently. However, skilled paddling techniques for turning a kayak under various wind and current conditions can usually offer the same benefits as a rudder.

Installing a rudder is not an easy task for someone who has never done it. It is a complicated process that takes three or four hours, even for someone who is practiced and has the right tools. As a general rule, have your favorite kayak shop install it for you, unless you enjoy solving mechanical problems. Third-party rudders can be particularly challenging since the kits are by nature very "generic" in order to be adaptable to every style of boat. If you decide to install a rudder yourself, consider asking the help of a friend who has already done it ... They will undoubtedly help you avoid a boat load of frustration.

Consider a rudder on your kayak ...
... If you buy a kayak that actually requires a rudder
Some kayaks, by virtue of their design or size, almost require the addition of a rudder system. The pros at your favorite kayak shop are aware of which kayak designs actually need a rudder for best performance. Longer kayaks or kayaks that have a hard time tracking in windy conditions will benefit from a rudder system. They can let you know if you are thinking about buying one of these kayaks.

... If your fishing style warrants a rudder
If you prefer to stay on top of the kayak to fish, a rudder can be a helpful tool for you. For instance, when drifting a shoreline throwing top water lures, the rudder can keep your boat angled properly to the shoreline, leaving you free to cast. You don't have to put down your rod and pick up your paddle to readjust your drift when a simple touch on the rudder footpeg will help counter the wind action.

If you generally fish the shallow back lakes and stalk the marshes you probably do not require a rudder. "Skinny" water, sand bars and heavily grassed flats can often make a rudder ineffective and sometimes a liability.

... If you intend to cross long distances of open water

Starting the day fighting a cross wind while paddling a couple of miles to fish is absolutely no fun. But, with a rudder on the kayak it's a much easier trek. A rudder keeps the kayak tracking in the direction that you want to go with a simple push of a toe on the foot peg, instead of fighting the turn with arm strength and a paddle. A rudder will get you to your destination with much less effort.

... If you are a "stuff" kind of angler who just wouldn't be satisfied without installing *everything* on a kayak

I know you are out there! If there's a kayak accessory available that you don't have yet, you won't rest until you have it.

That's OK ... enjoy your rudder!

You may NOT need a rudder on your kayak ...

... If you have a "mothership" craft to cross open water

If you have a motor boat that you load your kayak into to get to your fishing location, you can usually get away without a rudder. Since your motor boat is doing the work to cross open water and not you, there's less of a need for a rudder on your kayak. Also, loading and unloading a kayak with a rudder into your big boat can be tricky and the chance of breaking something on your rudder is always there.

... If you started kayak fishing to "keep it simple"

If you got involved with kayak fishing because of the simplicity it offers, you should think twice about that rudder. In the final analysis, a rudder is just another piece of gear that you must purchase, install, maintain and repair.

... If you have a tight budget

Having a rudder professionally installed on your kayak can cost an additional $200-$300 depending on your specific boat manufacturer and model. There are quality aftermarket rudders available out there, but they can often be even more expensive.

And a few other considerations ...

For fly fishermen, a clean cockpit area in your kayak is a must if you are using it as a stripping basket. Rudders are typically controlled by foot peg devices and the braces to support them and the odds are that your fly line will tangle around this gear when you are ready to cast at a fish. Some fly fishermen get around this by using a conventional stripping basket to contain their line.

Countless fish have been lost to the sharp edge of a rudder acting like a knife in the water behind the kayak. When fishing from your kayak and hooking fish, lift that rudder as soon as possible.

Proper "fit" for your kayak can ensure many hours of comfort and fun. Body type and fishing style are just a couple of factors to consider when getting your kayak.

Body type and Kayak size ...

There is really no "one size fits all" kayak and modern kayak manufacturers try to design models for all body types. Be honest about your abilities and strength ... you'll have more fun!

If you are Petite: Purchase a smaller, easier to handle kayak light enough to handle by yourself. If it's too big, too heavy or too bulky, you will likely get discouraged because it's just too much work.

If you are Heavy: Heavyweight paddlers have lots of choices in the sit-on-top kayak world. Remember, the wider the kayak the more stable it is. Add your weight and that of your gear and look at a kayak that is appropriate.

If you are Tall: If you are over 6' tall, make sure that your kayak has adequate leg space in the cockpit area for comfortable paddling. A tall person will also have a higher center of gravity. Picking a kayak that is too short could make it tippy because your center of gravity is not balanced by the length of the kayak.

Let's talk fishing style ...

If you primarily drift fish in your kayak (or rarely get out of your kayak to wade fish), comfort is top consideration ... choose a kayak comfortable for sitting over long periods of time. Look at longer kayaks which will allow you to cover more water with less effort. You may also want to have that rudder installed for ease of paddling the long distances and staying at the correct angle while drifting and casting to fishy shorelines.

A bright colored kayak is a safe kayak because it can easily be seen by other boaters

If you actually just use your kayak for transportation to your favorite fishing grounds and then get out and wade to your quarry, a fast, streamlined kayak could be the right choice for you. Go for length, storage space and definitely install a rudder.

If you stand up in your kayak, as more and more kayak anglers are preferring to do for sight-casting and fly casting, find a kayak that is wide and actually designed for standing up. Several manufacturers offer kayaks specifically for stand up fishermen.

Fly fishermen require a clean cockpit so that their fly lines don't get tangled up in gear, foot pegs, rod holders, and other gadgets. Consider this fact when purchasing a kayak for fly fishing.

If your main game is heading into the surf, choose a short, stable kayak that can turn on a dime between waves, and has the capacity to haul you and your gear out to the third bar and back.

Of course, if you are going to be transporting your kayak in your motor boat to your fishing destination, your first consideration would be to make sure it fits in the boat!

What About Color?

Another topic hotly debated! Aside from personal preference, the subject of color boils down to one issue ... **Safety.** Motor boats, airboats and other traffic traversing the shallow water and back lake marshes are concentrating on not getting stuck and trying to get to their fishing areas while watching the water and navigation aids. Since a kayaker is about alligator or log sized in the water, a camo, sand, granite or other naturally colored blend-in kayak lying low in the water will be hard to see. A fast moving boat with the bow up may completely overlook you and your kayak until it is too late ... Even if you do have the right of way! Consider the purchase of a bright colored kayak that everyone can see, including the Coast Guard from the air. The fish won't care and you never know when you might *actually need* help. Always better to be safe than sorry.

Overview

You've read the chapter and now have an idea in mind as to which kayak type might be best for you. Now check the boxes on the chart on the next page to take to your kayak dealer so they can steer you in the right direction.

My body type is: Small Medium Large X-Large	Some-times	No	Yes
I paddle long distances to fish			
I don't need to paddle very far to fish			
I use another boat to transport my kayak			
I like to fish from my kayak			
I like to get out and wade			
I like to fish the surf			
I stand up in my kayak & fish/sight cast			
I like to carry lots of gear			
I like to carry minimum gear			
I carry my kayak on a vehicle rack			
I carry my kayak in the back of my truck			
I carry my kayak on a trailer			
I wish somebody else would carry my kayak			

Notes to Self ...

Chapter 2

Rigging your kayak for fishing

Most kayak fishermen find their way into the perfectly rigged boat by just "doing" ... going out and fishing, seeing what they need, and where they need it installed and then making adjustments to their style of fishing ... it's a personal thing. Most new kayak fishermen rig out their kayaks like their buddies or at the recommendation of kayak retailers. This is an intelligent place to begin, but as you progress as a kayak angler, you will find through trial and error what really works for you and what doesn't. Part of the fun is getting to design your gear installations accordingly.

Firstly, you've got to have a seat and a paddle. Sound advice would be to spend the most you can afford on the most comfortable seat you can find. You'll be spending some long and hopefully pleasant hours there. If your back and rear aren't comfortable, you'll not want to spend time in your kayak. And purchase the lightest paddle that you can afford. There are a lot of choices out there using light-

Lightweight, self-contained and compact, modern kayaks allow sportsmen the opportunity to outfit their craft to match individual fishing preferences.

15

weight materials, ultra strong composites and proprietary designs. If your budget is tight, stick with a good quality generic paddle that feels good to your grip. You can always upgrade later for something more custom ... plus that first paddle will make a great spare.

Paddles

There are a variety of paddles on the market built with a wide range of materials. They all do the same thing ... Move your kayak. Some do it by requiring more effort than others. The main thing is weight. Light weight, ergonomic bends in the shaft, adjustable lengths and even different sized blades all contribute to the paddle being a custom tool. They can range in cost from $50 on up. Here are some of the details and differences to pay attention to.

Shafts are offered in a variety of materials. Aluminum and aluminum coated shafts tend to be least expensive but are also usually the heaviest aside from that old wooden paddle retrieved from the rafters in the garage. They are durable, long lasting and resistant to normal punishment. Fiberglass shafts are lighter and a little more expensive than aluminum and are comfortable on your hands. Carbon blends and composites are extremely light, extremely strong and just slightly less expensive than all-carbon models. All carbon fiber paddles are ultra light, and for some of us, ultra expensive.

The same general advice goes for blade materials. Plastic is sturdy, heavier, and the least expensive. The fiberglass and fiberglass blends are lighter than plastic, are plenty sturdy and offer mid-range pricing. Carbon blends and all carbon blades are expensive, tough and weigh almost nothing.

There are lots of theories out there about paddle length. Some of the things that need to be taken into consideration are torso height, width of the boat and your style of paddling. A lower stroke angle will generally require a longer paddle. At rest your hands should be placed about two thirds between the center of the shaft and the shoulder of the blade. Basically, if you have a wide kayak, you will need a longer paddle even if you are a short person. A 240 cm (about 4 feet) paddle is a good length for most applications. Fast, narrow kayaks can utilize a slightly shorter paddle (220cm) and a 230cm paddle is about the mid-range for sit-on-tops.

Width of Kayak

	Less than 24"	24" to 28"	28" and wider
Your height is under 5 ft. 5 in.	210-220 cm	230 cm	230-240 cm
Your height is 5 ft. 5 in. to 6 ft.	220 cm	230 cm	230-240 cm
Your height is 6 ft. or taller	220-230 cm	230-240 cm	240 cm

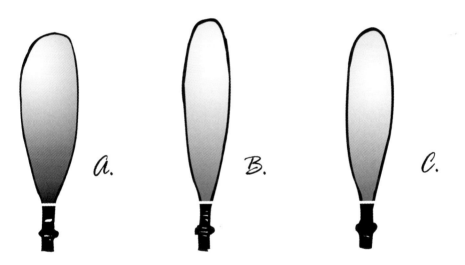

A. B. C.

Paddle shape A is a good general use paddle suitable for most applications, especially in shallow water or rough water. Paddle shape B is a longer, thinner blade which offers less wind resistance for long paddle trips yet has good bite for deeper waters. Paddle shape C is a thinner, shorter blade, but more streamlined than A. Because of it's smaller shape, it offers less resistance to wind and water and allows the paddler to actually paddle at a faster rate.

Seats

The number one requirement in a seat for an adult paddling a kayak is comfort. Find a seat that fits your rear and the length of your back as you sit in the kayak. Don't buy a seat until you sit in it to make sure that it hits your shoulders in a comfortable spot. If you are a short person and you purchase a super tall backed seat, it might be uncomfortable on your shoulders and neck. On the opposite end of the spectrum, if you are tall and you buy a seat that hits you in the middle of the back, it might not give you the back support necessary and become a torture after a short time on the water. Seats range in cost from $25 on up. Some kayak manufacturers have begun to build plastic seat-backs into their kayaks. In some cases, this will offer some initial cost savings since you can avoid buying an additional snap-on seat. But the Captain Sally recommendation is to be prepared to spend the money on a good seat in any case. You'll probably go back and buy one after you've paddled for any length of time with the plastic built-in seat back.

A quick rundown of the seats available on the market shows some basic divisions. Band back seats and halfback seats are minimum gear ... Inexpensive, but with no real support or booty cushion. Extra cushions, both of stick on foam and inflatable type cushions are available. Anyone who spends a lot of time paddling a kayak will enjoy a little extra cushioning in this area. Three-fourths seats are suitable for shorter people when a full backed seat reaches uncomfortably high. Full back seats and Gel cushion seats are pretty much the road that most adults choose. A high-quality, comfortable seat such as this will be in the $100 and up price range.

Some seats have rod holders built into them. If your kayak setup is compact and doesn't have adequate space to install rod holders,

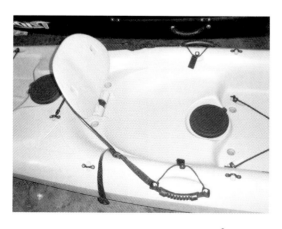

Built in seat backs are economical but not comfortable for day long trips

18

this may be a good alternative. Rod holders behind your seat back will make your rods a little hard to reach at times, but, if that's your only choice, it will work just fine.

If your seat is not properly adjusted, it will not be comfortable and it will not give you the support you need so take a little time to get your seat "set" properly. Most kayak seats have at least two adjustment points in the seat area and the

Some kayak seats have rod holders or storage built into them.

back area. After you have clipped the seat to your kayak, adjust all of the straps so that the seat cushion area does not slip down toward the center of the kayak and that the seat back area gives you enough support when you sit on the seat. The back rest should hold your back upright in a natural position and so that your rear does not slide away toward the middle of the kayak as you lean back.

Rod Holders

Having a rod holder (or holders) on your kayak makes a lot of sense. They keep your rods in place and ready for you to grab at a seconds notice. Rod holder placement is a personal decision ... I

Flush mounted rod holders are very handy.

place my rod holders right behind my seat, but some people like to have a rod holder mounted right in front of them. If you are a fly fisherman, you will need a specialty rod holder that accommodates a fly rod. Spinning and casting fisherman can use either a flush mount (mount goes inside of the boat hull) or a deck-mount bracket with a removable holder. Flush mounted rod holders take a bit of expertise to install. Unless you are the handy type, it is usually better to let your kayak shop do it since they are experienced. A rod leash is a good idea as well, especially when traveling long distances or through rough water where your rod might be bounced out of it's holder.

Anchors

An anchor is another essential piece of gear for kayak fishermen and there are several types on the market in different weights. The type of anchor you choose is also a personal decision, based on your style of fishing. There are several popular choices available.

An appropriate length of line, for shallow water fisherman somewhere between 6' to 12', braided directly to the anchor with a clip braided on the kayak end is a good way to ensure that your knot-tying won't fail and thereby lose your anchor ... or your boat.

Some kayak fishermen rig a pulley system that can allow the anchoring point to be adjusted to different angles on the side of your kayak. Rig your anchor this way if you enjoy staying in your kayak and fishing, more than getting out and wade fishing.

The folding anchor on the right is very popular because of its ease of storage and secure holding power on most type of bottom. The drift anchor on the left is for slowing the boat's drift under windy conditions and acts much like an underwater parachute.

Gear Storage

Most kayaks have some storage areas built into the hull which are suitable for items that you want to have with you at all times (your safety kit, foul weather gear, etc.) but don't necessarily need to be gotten into. Kayak dry bags are essential for storing all of these items in the hull of your boat. Even though these areas are technically "dry", they form condensation and your stuff can get damp.

Some kayak fishermen like to use a milk crate type container that fits into the storage well area behind the seat of most sit-on-top kayaks. This container keeps most of your tackle at hand such as your anchor and other gear, plus can accommodate rod holders, etc. Gear storage methods and all others are personal preferences and depend on your type of fishing. The Captain Sally way is to keep things simple, which

Dry bags come in a variety of styles and sizes ... Dry is Good!

is the reason most of us went to kayak fishing to begin with, so I don't clutter up the cockpit or the tank well of my kayak with anything unnecessary.

Small tackle boxes, tackle organizers or plastic partitioned containers can hold appropriate selections of lures, hooks, plastic baits and spoons without taking up a lot of space. Waterproof boxes keep tackle dry and salt-free ... And they float. Go ahead and trim down ... leave your gigantic tackle box on wheels in the truck and take only what you'll need for your day.

Another piece of fishing gear you might wish to consider is a GPS. A GPS is essential for kayak fishermen, either hand-held or mounted on your kayak. A knowledgeable user will never be lost. But even a knowledgeable user will be lost without batteries ... Be sure that you have spares. This item is discussed in more detail in the Safety Chapter of this book.

Fishermen who kayak and fish in deeper bays may wish to install a depth finder. This is a good tool for finding reefs and obstructions. It is essential that the transducer be mounted properly for the instrument to work correctly so be sure to consult with an experienced installer before putting one on your kayak. Find a waterproof model for the ultimate protection and have lots of spare batteries on board if you rely on this gear to find fish.

Gear and tackle storage are personal preferences. Keep it simple, keep it dry and keep it light. Remember ... You are the paddling engine!

Chapter 3

Putting it all together.

What
TO TAKE
& How to Take It

Now that you've purchased your kayak, seat and paddle, one of the toughest parts about going on a kayak fishing trip is deciding what to take and how to take it. Most people who start kayak fishing were previously shoreline waders or boat fishermen. These anglers are notorious for their tremendous lure assortments. But now it's time to whittle down that giant over-the-shoulder tackle bag with the 12 separate lure and worm cases into a manageable and kayakable tackle assortment!

Fly fisherman already know how to put together a small selection of essentials. A well thought-out fly box with a dozen or so flies to match the seasonal natural baits, a spare leader, a small spool of tippet material, clippers and pliers or hemostats all will fit into a wading pack, lightweight vest or even a shirt pocket. Lure fishermen, on the other hand, have a slightly different "problem". With very little coaxing, they might show off an entire room at their house dedicated to tackle and lures in all sizes, colors and styles.

The reason you went to a kayak was probably to pare down a little, get simpler with your fishing, get shallow and get away from the crowded shorelines. This is your chance ... I'm going to try to make you feel a little bit better about leaving behind 15 of your favorite 20 topwater choices as you paddle away to your fishing destination!

The Right Stuff

Let's start with safety. For most fishermen, safety is an afterthought, but a kayak fisherman needs to place safety first. A kayak fisherman is self-propelled, self-contained and most likely far away from the support of either boat or truck. If something hap-

A rod leash can easily pay for itself the first time you use it!

23

pens out on the water, you could be in a real jam if you don't have the right stuff. Everyone **must** have a personal flotation device ... always have it ready. Wear it at all times if you are crossing deep water or if you get caught in bad weather.

The second thing everyone should do is to put together a dry bag "safety kit". A generic kayak dry bag may be found at most outdoor shops and all kayak specialty shops. These bags are made specifically for kayakers and boaters. A little later in the book is a list of "must have" basics for any kayak safety kit.

You really need a supportive seat. We've already talked about seats in an earlier chapter. Do not save money on a seat ... your back will let you know you've made the wrong decision!

Every kayak needs an anchor and hopefully you have already purchased one. My anchor has about 6 feet of line and a snap clip on the end of the line to securely attach it to my kayak. My anchor choice is a 3 lb. grappling-type anchor. With this anchor, I know I won't be chasing my kayak if a big wind blows up in the middle of the afternoon! Some kayakers rig a pulley system to position their anchor or drift anchor properly to the wind. If you are mostly fishing from your kayak, this might be a good way to operate your anchor. If you are using your kayak mainly for transportation and then getting out to wade to your fish, attach your anchor with a short piece of line to a point near the middle of your kayak so that your boat will swing around less in the wind.

Rod holders are essential. If you only fish with conventional tackle, a flush mount rod holder will work just great. Mount two on your kayak so that you can carry a couple of rods rigged with different lures. If you are a fly fisherman, a deck-mounted fly-rod holder is essential. Mount the rod holders where they won't be in your way, but where you can reach them in a hurry when you need to. Fly fishermen need to keep their kayak cockpits relatively clutter-free, so don't mount rod holders where your line may be prone to tangling in it.

A paddle leash can save you money and possibly a long wade home.

A handy way to attach your paddle to you kayak is with a paddle leash. If you see some fish and want to get out and wade them, a paddle leash will allow you

24

to silently leave your paddle floating in the water beside your boat. And, if the wind picks up and blows the paddle off your kayak while you are out wading, you can still get home because your paddle will still be there. This is a very cheap insurance policy, as paddles can range from $100 to $400!

As a guide, I both fly fish and throw lures in the shallows, so I have 2 small canvas bags which hold multiple plastic boxes of fishing tackle, one for lure fishing, one for fly fishing.

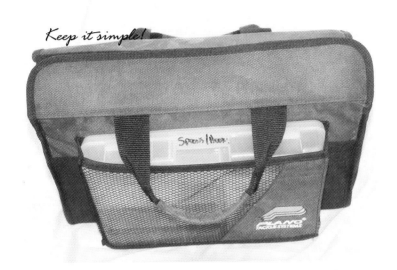

Organize your tackle by type, such as "top waters", "spoons", "soft plastics", "misc.", etc. Each category might merit its own partitioned plastic box within your tackle bag. Within each box, organize your lures and plastics by color. That way, at a glance, you can see if you are running low on your favorite color!

Besides your tackle and fly selections, include clippers, pliers, hemostats, wading belt and a stringer and you are ready to catch fish! If not fishing "catch and release", bring along a second soft-sided cooler filled with ice for your fish. It can be stored in the dry well of your kayak. Dragging your fish behind you all day is, in the very least, a work out! More importantly, your fish will die and possibly spoil. It's amazing how many fish you can fit into a small soft-sided cooler!

It seems almost too simple, but one of the more important items you should make part of your rig is a length of line tied to the bow of your kayak. At the end of this line, or at both ends if you prefer, put a strong snap clip. You can pull your boat along behind you by just clipping it to your wading belt, you can tie off your boat to keep it from drifting, or in a situation that requires towing, you have a tow line. Keep it light and manageable.

Other items you might want to carry with you will be a pair of binoculars and a map of the area you are fishing. Aerial photograph maps are handy to help you weave your way through the islands and sloughs of the back lakes. If you are savvy about electronics, a hand-held, waterproof GPS will keep track of where you've been and let you backtrack out. A GPS will also help you to mark the various "secret spots" you'll encounter as you become more familiar with the fishing territory.

I keep mentioning this, but the most important thing about kayak fishing is to be safe. Let people know where you are going to be kayaking, take a cell phone or other means of communication, pare down your gear and have a good time! Not only will you catch fish, but, as you gain experience and confidence, you will enjoy natural peace and quiet as you move farther and farther off the beaten path ... See you there!

For a week ... or a weekend. Plan and pack accordingly.

Chapter 4

What to wear

It wouldn't seem that the clothes and shoes that you wear would be that important in kayak fishing, but they are! Wearing the right clothes and accessories will definitely make your trip more comfortable, productive, protective and enjoyable.

Let's start with footwear and the right kind of wading boots. Absolutely avoid wearing tennis shoes, sandals, water shoes and the like as they provide no foot protection of any kind from sharp shell, sucking mud or obstructions. Even if you don't intend to leave your kayak to walk or wade, there is always a chance that you will be forced to. Always wear the appropriate footwear. In the event that you paddle into an area where the water is too shallow and you have

Proper outdoor wear can make the difference between a memorable trip and a miserable one. It seems counter-intuitive, but long sleeve shirts are actually cooler!

to get out and walk, you will have the right gear for the job. There are several types of saltwater wading boots available, but any good boot will do. A boot that protects the bottom of your feet and that is comfortable is probably the most important accessory you can own next to good glasses. Wearing a pair of lightweight microfiber or polyester socks (like ski boot liners) in your wading boots helps to keep feet protected from rubbing against the insides of the boots and keeps feet feeling relaxed and comfortable as they slide around. Your feet will feel less fatigued after a day of wading when you wear lightweight, slippery socks in your boots.

Kayak fishermen, by the nature of the sport, are particularly susceptible to stingray hits. Fishing extreme shallow water, jumping in and out of the kayak, fishing "side-saddle" with both of your legs dangling off of one side of the kayak and wadefishing really up the odds of getting hit by a stingray. Stingray boots can definitely be a good investment. A hit by a stingray will surely end your day, not to mention a week or maybe a month of fishing. A stingray episode also demands a trip to the hospital since a marine infection left untreated can cause a great deal of damage and result in a wound that resists healing. So, for between $65 to $130 you can wear an insurance policy against the potential of this very painful and expensive saltwater incident. But they only work if you wear them. I have been wearing them since they came on the market.

No cotton and no t-shirts!

Cotton shirts will absorb salt and spray and stay wet longer than synthetic fabrics. Cotton does not offer much protection from the sun either. If you really want to be comfortable on a kayak, investigate SPF or UPF nylon or polyester micro-fiber fabrics. Because they're designed to not hold moisture and to dry very quickly, they have the effect of actually keeping you cool. Not only should your shirts be quick dry, so should your shorts, pants and jackets. All outdoor wear is now available in these fabrics. Also make sure that your clothing has lots of easily accessible pockets. Just as there is no such

Dressed for success ...

thing as having too much drinking water or too much ice ... you can't have too many pockets! They'll keep everything within reach at all times.

Go natural ... not white! Kayak fishing allows the angler to be a uniquely stealthy, sneaky fisherman. Because you are getting so close to the fish, it's important that you wear colors that don't reflect an unnatural glare toward the water. White shirts can have the effect of making the fisherman appear as a large bright predator splashing towards the fish and they will flee from the reflection. Try to wear colors that blend in with the surrounding habitat such as light blue, khaki, tan, or green.

Long sleeves, even in the heat of midsummer will actually keep you cooler on hot days. Keeping the sun off of your arms, keeping a good ventilation through your shirt, and the evaporation of the water from the surface of your microfiber shirt will make you feel cooler than bare skin baking in the sun. At first, I had a hard time believing this, but have worn long-sleeved shirts for the past ten years.

Long pants will protect your legs from sunburn, stinging jellyfishes of all types, mud bugs, flies and other leg irritants that live in the water and grass. New kayakers that like to wear shorts are easy to spot because of their unnatural walk. Sitting on that new kayak means a real uncomfortable sunburn on the inside part of your thigh that doesn't see much sun! Bring a pair of pants, and if you are wearing shorts while kayaking, don't forget to sunscreen the inside parts of your thighs or you'll be walking funny for a few days after your trip ... Not exactly a great souvenir!

Hats ... Your Portable Shade Tree

A hat is just about as important as every other item that you'll wear on your kayak fishing trip. It protects your head and face from the sun, keeps you dry when it rains, and is a handy place to stick an extra lure. It can portray your feelings about life, your personal style or even the companies you do business with. A hat keeps your hair under control or your bald spot from frying like bacon. Whether you choose a basic baseball cap (watch out for the top of your ears), a wide-brimmed sombrero, a snappy Aussie soft brim or a Foreign Legion style with protective neck cape, make sure that the under side of the brim is a dark color to cut glare reflected up from the water. Your eyes will thank you for it at the end of the day. And if your favorite fishin' hat has a light colored underbrim, don't worry, customizing with a good old-fashioned marker pen should take care of it!

About Sunglasses ...

The subject of sunglasses could be an entire chapter in the book! The debate is hot ... Color, shape, price range, and so forth. For a beginning sight caster, a pair of polarized sunglasses is not optional, it is essential. Without them, "seeing" fish under the water or understanding important bottom contours is impossible. If you can afford it, buy a pair of glasses with quality scratch resistant lenses. The price range for a pair of these polarized sunglasses is about $100-$200. These glasses should be considered every bit as important as a good rod, the right lure or fly or new line on your reel. Inexpensive

Rosy vermillion or light brown amber are good all-round lense choices

polarized glasses purchased at your local sporting goods outlet, while filling the need, generally do not have the durability and quality that the top market brands do. Inexpensive glasses are, however, usually less painful to lose overboard. Buy the most expensive sunglasses you can afford, and make sure they have polarized lenses. Get a comfortable strap to keep them around your neck ... a floating strap is good. Quality polarized sunglasses are a tool ... one of **the** most important tools for a sight-caster and a fisherman. Just as a qualified mechanic wouldn't think of purchasing his tools from the dollar bin at a discount store, neither should the serious fisherman and kayaker skimp on fishing tools!

Lens color is important. Early morning light, hazy or foggy conditions require high contrast to see through the water. Under these conditions, use yellow tinted lenses. During the early part of the day, after sunrise but before the sun is high above your head, vermillion (rosy colored), amber or brown lenses will afford the best contrast. If you can afford the luxury of owning more than one pair of sunglasses, then you may have the full spectrum of lens colors appropriate for each time of the day. But if you are looking for a good utility sunglass color for all conditions, pick the rosy shade of vermillion or a light brown amber. These colors offer good contrast under almost all conditions.

A good fitting pair of sunglasses that keeps side light out will reduce squinting and eye strain. Individually wrapped lens cleaner wipes that you can buy in the optical department of any grocery store are a valuable addition. These are moistened with a solution that will care for your good lenses. Also, if it rains and your dry cloth gets wet, or if you wind up with salt spray on your lenses, you'll always have a way to keep your glasses clean. Keep a few in your pocket at all times.

Foul weather gear, jackets and dressing in layers

Foul weather gear is essential kayak gear. You never know when a storm is going to blow through, a cold wind or rain or a fog bank will roll in. Without the right gear to protect you from the elements, even in the heat of middle summer you could suffer hypothermia. A set of foul weather gear that can be folded into a small package is best. There are several manufacturers that offer rain gear made from "space-age" material that is lightweight, breathable, and won't mold or crack. They can be crushed into a ball and be stuffed into a dry bag to be always handy when needed. Never leave your truck or boat without your jacket and pants.

For winter kayaking prepare by dressing in layers. Start out with lightweight silk or microfiber shirts and pants like you would wear under your suit when snow skiing. Then add a long-sleeved shirt, fleece jacket and warm, breathable wading jacket. Find a jacket that is short, and preferably has a rubberized cuff around the wrists that can be adjusted to stop cold water from dribbling down into your shirt. Long-underwear liner pants, along with a fleece pair of pants that fit comfortably and warm under breathable waders will allow for easy movement. From the Captain Sally point of view, I always wear a snug-fitting belt around the waist of my waders just in case I fall down. From a safety standpoint, this will stop most of the water from pouring into your waders.

If you dress in easy to peel layers, you'll have more fun, be more comfortable and be able to maintain comfort and agility in almost any fishing and weather conditions.

The Layered Look is In!
...And plenty warm.

Chapter 5

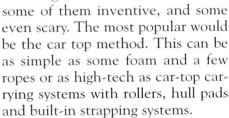

Getting to the Water

Now that you've found your ideal kayak and you've rigged it out for fishing, getting your kayak to the water will be your next challenge. You have probably noticed a great many ways to haul kayaks,

some of them inventive, and some even scary. The most popular would be the car top method. This can be as simple as some foam and a few ropes or as high-tech as car-top carrying systems with rollers, hull pads and built-in strapping systems.

The most important aspect to consider when hauling your kayak to the water is your ease of use. You can have the most expensive roof top system on market, but if it's too hard or frustrating to use, you just won't use it very often. If your kayak fishing trip begins with cussing, sweating and back pain while loading up your kayak to get it to the water, chances are that your kayak fishing career will be very short-lived.

Vehicle top rack systems

There are several high-end car/SUV top systems on the market today which are easily adapted to your type of vehicle. Perhaps one of the most sophisticated will lower down from your roof so that

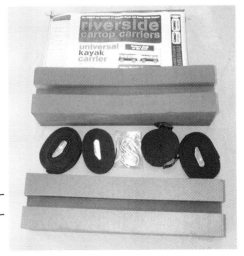

Simple universal kayak carriers can meet most needs of those without pickup trucks.

you can easily load your kayak into the rack. Then, with the click of a button, a hydraulic lift moves your kayak from the side of your vehicle to the top. Several manufactures have customized systems that are available in all price ranges. Most of these systems are installed by the store you buy them from. Make sure that you fully understand loading and tying the kayaks to the rack system.

If you are on a budget, there are a few manufacturers that make universal foam block systems that work just great. These systems even come with all of the straps you need to haul your kayak safely tied to the roof of your vehicle. Whatever your budget, roof top transportation methods are safe, efficient for traveling, and come in many types and styles.

However, if you are single handedly loading your kayak on the roof of your vehicle, especially if it's a tall SUV, it may be challenging to get it up there without a struggle. If you will be hauling your kayak single handedly most of the time, you may want to opt for another style of transporting your kayak, like a pull-behind trailer. This is especially handy for two or more kayaks.

Easy to load and unload, a small trailer is often a good choice for two or more kayaks

If you choose to haul your kayaks on a trailer, you can really get elaborate. Trailer rack systems and locking storage boxes can be easily rigged to haul your stuff to the water. Since trailers are low to the ground, getting kayaks off of the trailer and down to the water is really easy. Kayak trailers are lightweight and can be attached, via a receiver hitch, to most small cars and trucks.

Loading your kayak over the top

Roof top mounting systems don't get any easier!

of your pickup truck bed is an efficient way to travel since you can still use the bed of your truck to haul all of your other stuff. Several truck manufacturers now offer their own kayak rack systems. The same companies that sell rooftop transportations systems also sell truck rack systems. Hauling your kayak(s) on a rack that extends over your cab and over the truck bed, leaves your truck bed completely available for the storage of the rest of your camping, kayak and fishing stuff.

Hauling your kayak in the back of your pickup is just about as easy as it can get. Add a red flag to whatever is sticking out over the tailgate, wrap a few tie-straps around the kayak and the tailgate and secure the front of your kayak to any tie-down mounted in the bed of your truck and you can safely and securely get fishing without much expense or frustration. Some longer kayaks, however, may need an extension system to keep them level and secure. This also keeps the kayak from flexing or bending in the wrong place. Most of these extensions attach to the receiver hitch on your truck. The most important aspect of hauling your kayak to the water, which ever way you choose to do it, is to tie them down properly.

Fisherman's luck means that the time, the place, the fish and you are all together. It does not happen very often.

Zane Grey

Chapter 6

Paddling your kayak

Control your stroke! Being relaxed and holding the paddle correctly will increase your paddle stroke power. Your arms should remain relaxed and your elbows should be bent, not extended. This position prevents your arms from becoming overextended. Paddle strokes should be done with your arms positioned comfortably in front of your body like the front legs of a kangaroo. All paddle strokes combine both a push with one arm, and a pull with the other. Your control hand holds the paddle shaft with the top of your hand lined up with the top of the paddle blade. Keeping your hands aligned correctly while pushing with your top hand and pulling with your bottom hand will make it easy to move your paddle through the water. A little practice will go a long way. A common paddling error while beginning is holding the paddle shaft with a death grip. This will wear you out in a hurry and is ineffective for a full day of paddling. Remember to relax the non-control hand during every paddle stroke.

After a little experience, you will find your most efficient and best "all day" stroke.

Show me the power!

Strokes begin by understanding two important principles. First, it is your torso (your core body), not your arms that is the primary source of power. Second, a good, secure hand position on the paddle shaft and a relaxed arm position are necessary before making any stroke movement.

Your torso is the main generator of power, which then transfers the power to your arms and hands, which then transfers the power to your blade in the water. Skipping the power of the torso is like not using your legs to lift something heavy. Without using your whole body to establish a good paddling rhythm, you'll wind up with tired arms and ineffective paddling strokes.

To start off, get a good controlling grip with the top hand on your paddle shaft. Rotate your whole upper body slightly as you dip your paddle blade into the water near your foot and draw your paddle blade toward the back of the boat with a slow and steady movement. Push with your top hand and pull with your bottom hand. Lift your blade out of the water at the end of the stroke near the back of your boat and begin again on the other side of the kayak.

Moving with deliberation in this style will provide an efficient use of your paddling stroke. Keeping your blade fully in the water while drawing it from the front of the kayak to the back of the kayak and avoiding any extraneous movement or splashing will keep you efficiently paddling all day long. It takes a little time to find the right individual cadence and rhythm, but the end result is a comfortable day on the water and not an exhausting one.

On very windy days, using these basic techniques can be even more important. Keep your paddle positioned at a low angle to the water. Paddling directly into the wind is always easier than moving a kayak sideways to the wind since you offer less surface resistance. Keep as low as possible to keep from acting like a sail. Slow, steady motions, while keeping lower to the water will help to move your kayak into a strong wind.

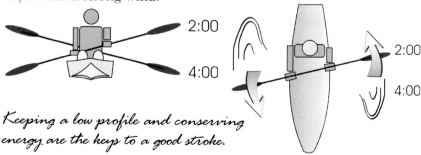

Keeping a low profile and conserving energy are the keys to a good stroke.

Chapter 7
Weather, Safety & Communication

Weather Safety and COMMUNICATION

There's a lot of freedom on the water and all of us love the great fishing that kayaking provides. Being prepared on the water is the responsibility of every boater, but if you are kayaking, it becomes even more important. Being self-propelled and self-contained, a kayak fisherman has a few more things to think about. Have fun on the water fishing from your kayak, but be prepared just in case something goes wrong.

File a "float plan" so people will know where you are. Map out your plan for the day, know where you are going and how to tell someone where you are. Call your spouse or friends and let them know your general vicinity and the approximate time you will return. If help is needed, that contact person can send help in your direction. Better yet, a waterproof, hand held GPS (about $130) will give your rescuers exact coordinates of your location. If you turn it on at the beginning of your trip, it will help you backtrack out to safety should you be caught in a fog or blinding rain or get lost.

Bad weather is inevitable ... be prepared. There is no kayak in this picture!

Wear your PFD. It is the law that you must have a PFD handily available on your kayak at all times. If you are crossing deep water, or if the wind or weather make you feel uncomfortable, put the PFD on. It will save your life. Your PFD should be comfortable and fit you properly. Attach your whistle to your PFD so you will be in total compliance with Texas Parks and Wildlife Department regulations.

Always take your kayak safety kit with you whenever you get into your kayak.

Take appropriate communication gear with you. Buy a waterproof hand held VHF radio for emergency communications. Have extra batteries with you. A cell phone is good, but if it gets wet, it stops working (you should carry your cell phone in a waterproof case that you can talk through). You may well be out of range of any towers and have no signal. A waterproof hand held VHF radio is a sure way to communicate with the Coast Guard or someone else on the water that can help you.

Pay attention! Before leaving for the day, check all available sources of weather information, especially if you suspect that there is weather approaching. Don't rely on the weather reports from the night before. VHF radios have up-to-date weather information on specific weather bands that run constantly ... Another good reason to have a VHF with you. Set the weather band to automatically announce weather warnings during the day and there will be less of a chance that unpredicted or developing weather will catch you off guard. Keep an eye to the sky. Wind direction changes can be harbingers of impending weather changes. Don't ignore thunder, dark clouds or cool winds. Go with your gut feelings. If you think things are changing, they probably are. Be ready to react.

Use Maps and Charts. Unless you've been fishing a particular area since you were born, you will certainly need to utilize maps and charts. Fishing maps that offer basic information such as the type of bottom conditions, wade fishing locations, kayak launch points and so forth are indispensable for a kayak fisherman embarking into a new fishing location. Aerial maps are especially helpful when fishing back lake and marsh areas. Aerial maps show details such as water depth (darker water), sand bars (lighter water), paddling passes and the overall "big picture" of your fishing spot. This type of map is invaluable to understanding the water flow and potential fishing approach to a marsh, lake or estuary. Kayak fishermen should find aerial maps for all of their favorite fishing places.

Consulting current aerial maps will help you to navigate the back country waters.

Always have foul weather gear with you on your kayak. Who would think about hypothermia in South Texas? Weather changes can bring cold rain and wind. If you are forced to wait out a storm sitting in a duck blind or on a shoreline, you can be assured that your body temperature will start to drop. Fight the possibility of hypothermia with the appropriate rain gear and be sure to put these on before you get soaked to the skin. Keep a space blanket or a space sleeping bag, available at any outdoor retailer, in your safety bag. They're small and very light, easy to find and will be most welcome should you actually have to use them.

A bright colored kayak can save your life. You will be spotted quickly by a rescuer if necessary, but more importantly, by other boaters. There have been many scary stories recounted to me from power boaters and kayakers alike that have had near-collisions with each other. Kayakers, if you don't have a brightly colored kayak and you are paddling narrow sloughs or tiny lakes, put up a flag so power boaters under way can see you in advance. Technically, a kayak has the right of way, but if a power boater doesn't see you or refuses to give you some space, don't be so foolish as to risk your life for the principal that you have a right to be there too. Get out of the way. Put your paddle up into the air and let the boater know you exist.

More and more kayakers are paddling shared areas and it's just a matter of time until there is a kayak and power boat collision. You don't need to be that statistic.

Always take your kayak safety kit with you whenever you get into your kayak. A medium-sized dry bag filled with the following gear will serve you well under most conditions. Stow it in your kayak and don't leave home without it!

The Basic Kayak Safety Kit

Waterproof hand-held VHF radio with weather bands
Cell phone with waterproof bag

First aid kit (waterproof)	Whistle and a horn
Bright colored flag or flare kit	Waterproof hand-held GPS
Spare batteries	Space solar blanket
Multi-tool (Leatherman type)	Waterproof flashlight
Signal mirror (or old CD)	Compass

4-piece emergency paddle or spare paddle

Good rain suit (top and pant)	Waterproof matches or lighter
Extra sunscreen	Water
Extra hat	Power bars/Snacks

Thermal pack heater/s (like skiers use) and a Tube sock

Power boats are required to have a small flare kit on board at all times and it's a good idea for a kayaker as well.

Most of this list makes perfect sense, there are some out there asking "what's with the tube sock and the ski thermal packs?" While wading the shallows and concentrating on tailing fish, a fellow angler got hit by a stingray. He made it back to his kayak but because of

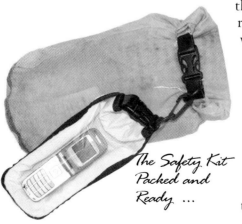

The Safety Kit Packed and Ready ...

the excruciating pain he had a really tough time paddling the way back to his truck. At the hospital, a very wise doctor recommended that he take a tube sock and a couple of skiing thermal packs with him from now on. The heat from the packs breaks down toxins left by the stingray's barb and helps diminish the pain. The tube sock can hold the pack in place on the wound while you get back to your vehicle. This sounded like great advice, so I've included it on my essentials list. All of these items will fit in a small to medium-sized dry bag and can be stowed away in your dry compartment on your kayak. Don't leave home without it, no matter how short your trip may be. If you don't have a dry compartment, strap it across the back of your kayak. And it is always a good idea to take a cooler with plenty of water and ice and include some snacks so you won't run out of energy midday.

One of *the* most important things to take along with you on a kayak fishing trip is a cool head. When things get tough and you feel that survival preparations may be necessary, don't panic. People that panic make the wrong decisions, and that could mean life or death. Get to a safe place and stay there. Make a shelter (an overturned kayak makes a great shelter). Gather your necessary safety items around you. Use your tools to get help. Don't take chances. Being self-contained and self-propelled, kayakers need to think about things a little differently. This independence on the water makes kayaking very appealing for all outdoors people. Here's your opportunity to set the pace to be safe and responsible. Pressure your friends to comply as well. Let's make kayak fishing one of the safest sports on the water.

... The Safety Kit revealed.

43

The charm of fishing is that it is the pursuit of what is elusive
but attainable ... a perpetual series of occasions for hope.

John Buchan

44

Chapter 8
Stuff Happens

When THINGS GO WRONG

Kayaking in the coastal back lakes or marshes, you are self contained and self propelled, out of your natural environment and at the hands of circumstances you can't control. And everyone knows you don't fool with Mother Nature. To be safe, you have to be prepared for anything and everything.

We've talked about overall safety in other parts of this book, but here are a few situations that all kayakers might face at one time or another. Here are a few pointers on how best to handle them.

Bad Weather ... It can happen at any time, especially along the Texas coast. Your post card perfect day takes a twist to the dark side as an unexpected squall approaches. If you've ever experienced this kind of surprise weather, you know how stressful it can become in a hurry. Lightning hits the water, the rain is blowing sideways and it's dark as dusk between the flashes. You are in your kayak, in the middle of nowhere and with no chance at getting to your boat or truck ... What should you do?

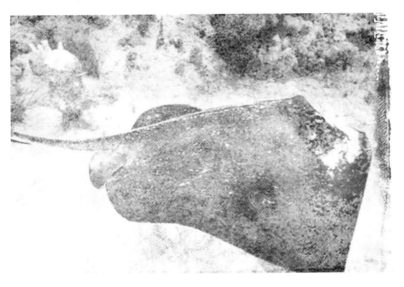

Captain Sally sez ... Do not step on these.

45

First things first. You need to make a calm assessment of the gravity of the situation. Is this the quick-moving front you saw on the weather last night or is it going to hang around a while. Is there lighting involved? Do you feel scared or threatened? These are all important factors in accessing whether you should make your way back to your truck or boat, or take cover and ride it out.

It's just the weather ...

It will change

Hang in there

Always err on the side of caution especially with lightning. In many cases, you and your kayak might be the tallest thing on the water. Take down your kayak flag and rod and reels and lay them flat. Work yourself to the bank. Get off the water on low ground if you can. Drag your kayak up on the land. Put your graphite or carbon paddles and rods on the ground away from your cover. Flip your kayak over and enjoy the relative dry underneath it ... you did bring a snack, didn't you?

Wait until it is absolutely safe to emerge. Generally speaking, it's better to be alive and wet than being hit by lightning while madly paddling your way back to your truck to take cover. My advice to you is find cover when weather approaches. It is weather ... it will change. Hang tight until the danger has passed.

If there is no dry ground around you, move up into the weeds or mangroves and flip your kayak over for shelter. Don't forget, hypothermia can always occur in a cold rain even in the summertime. If you are drenched and cold, sit down in the water under your kayak. Summer water temperatures are much warmer than the water falling from thousands of feet above. You can keep warm this way, although wet, while safely waiting out a long, cold rain event.

If you are out on an open flat, look for duck blinds around you. Paddle over and tie your kayak to the duck blind and get in. A duck blind will get you off of the water and are usually somewhat protected from the wind and rain. Get your rain gear out (if you haven't done do already) and put it on. Get your space blanket from your waterproof safety kit and wrap it around you. Enjoy your stay. Remind yourself ... *This is weather, it will change.*

The Coast Guard is always there monitoring Channel 16 to help you. If you are truly in distress in that there seems to be no end to the storm in sight and it's getting late in the day, or someone in your party is injured, or for any emergency whatsoever, don't hesitate to call the Coast Guard on your waterproof hand-held VHF radio. When you reach the Coast Guard, don't be chatty. Give them your name, the nature of your emergency, then give them your GPS position (from your waterproof hand-held GPS) and they will know exactly where to find you. Make sure you always have spare batteries in your waterproof safety kit for both of these devices. You never know when you will need them. This one simple preparation can make the difference between a great trip or tragedy.

Falling off of your kayak in deep water ... In a perfect world, you would have already practiced falling off of your kayak and then getting back on it in deep water. It makes sense to work on your techniques for re-entry before you have an emergency.

As with any emergency, the key to survival is not to panic. If you have fallen off of your kayak in deep water and can't get back on, simply hang on to your kayak and kick over to a safer or shallower place. Hopefully, if you were crossing deep water, you were wearing your PFD. If not, put it on! If your PFD is in a storage compartment on your kayak, this could present a very difficult challenge. Do whatever you can, safely and without panicking, to open that hatch and bring your PFD out and put it on as safely and calmly as possible. Don't turn loose of your boat! At this point, reflect as to how much easier it would have been to just wear it in the first place. Relax and catch your breath. Conserve your energy. You got yourself into this, and you are going to get yourself out of it!

If you are paddling your kayak across open and deep water, Always wear a PFD ... Period!

When you catch your breath and feel reenergized, it is time to attempt to get yourself back on your kayak. With your bow line or a piece of rope, tie your kayak to you in such a way that you don't get tangled, but so that it doesn't get away from you either. If you are wearing heavy wading boots, try and remove them. If you are unable to do so and you can't wiggle your way back on board, your best bet is to hang on to your kayak and just float until you either get help from someone, or you reach shallower water. The most important thing about this entire situation, is never, ever panic. The kayak floats ... you float ... stay with the kayak. A cool head will keep you alive until you figure out how to resolve your situation.

Stingray ... The "sting" of a stingray is actually a modified dermal denticle (the scales covering sharks and stingrays) with two side grooves filled with venom-producing tissue. The barb is surrounded

47

by a cell-rich covering or sheath that also produces lesser amounts of venom. The venom itself is a protein-based toxin that causes great pain in mammals and will generally alter heart rate and respiration. However, since it is a protein, it can be inactivated by exposure to high temperatures (about 120 degrees). Because of this, if you immerse the wound in hot water or apply a heat compress as an immediate treatment, this may reduce the initial pain of a stingray injury. The sting on most swimming stingrays is situated near the base of the tail. In nature, this may discourage predators from biting the animal near its vital organs. The sting of most bottom-dwelling stingrays is located further away from the body along the tail which makes it a more effective and dangerous "striking" weapon. However, it should be pointed out that the sting is purely a defensive weapon only, and that the "striking" action is an involuntary response rather than a real attack.

Although I have luckily never been hit by a stingray, I have been told that it is some of the worst pain you can feel. Some people can even pass out, and if you do not seek medical attention immediately, you will undoubtedly get a marine infection. This infection could cause serious healing complications, keep you off the water, cost you a ton of money and be painful for a long time.

Needless to say, the best way to handle a stingray hit is to avoid it completely by wearing the appropriate stingray proof boots and/or guards. Some people do not care for the guards because of the bulk, or because of the noise in the water when wading or other personal reasons. Most stingray accidents happen when a fisherman is backing up and fighting a fish and steps on the ray, or in deep water or in heavy grass where bottom is hard to see. You can usually avoid the problem by keeping alert and walking the "stingray shuffle", but if

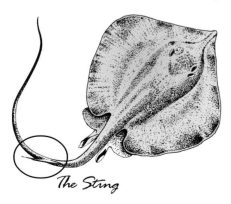

The Sting

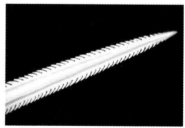

The Barb, up close and personal. You can see why you can't just "pull it out"

48

you are one of the unlucky folks who get tagged by a stingray, there are a few specific things that you can do to help with the pain while you make your way to the hospital.

If you are alone, go ahead and demand loudly why such a creature was ever created ... cuss a little. Everybody does. But, remain as calm as possible. Make your way back to your kayak and be prepared for your body to go into shock. Each person has different levels of fitness and tolerance ... it is not uncommon to pass out, so just as soon as you get into your kayak, grab your waterproof safety kit and lay back. Get out your cell phone and call for help. Let people know where you are and how long it may take you to paddle out. If you don't feel as though you can paddle out by yourself, ask someone to come in and get you. Give them your GPS coordinates and your general location immediately. Wash the wound with drinking water, not sea water. Sea water contains too many bacteria. Contrary to popular myth, vinegar or urine do not help ... the toxin does not break down easily to acids. Heat can definitely help to alleviate the pain of a stingray hit, so a thermal pack similar to the kind that you would use when skiing to keep your feet warm, may just help. The initial sharp pain lasts from 30 to 60 minutes and becomes more of a dull ache after that. If you can't get in touch with a friend on the land to come help and you feel that you can't paddle back out to your vehicle or boat, call the Coast Guard on VHF Channel 16. Give them your name, your emergency and your GPS position and wait for help. Then, get to a hospital immediately.

Be Smarto Not Macho. Seek medical attention!!

If you are with someone, hail your fishing partner just as soon as you get hit. They might already be able to tell from the shouting, splashing and hopping around that something has happened, but go ahead and let them know that you need their help. Proceed as before. At this point, however, your fishing buddy can put your kayak in tow and paddle you out to safety. Have your friend take you to the emergency room so you can be treated immediately for the pain, infection and any other complications that might occur. A stingray barb not only has a toxic slime on it, but it is very difficult to remove without leaving pieces in the wound. It is very important to understand that medical attention for a stingray hit should be sought immediately. Marine infections can be deadly, and in the very least, can cause severe pain and long-term wound healing difficulties. This is not the time to be macho. Be mucho smarto ... Seek medical attention.

A word about Vibrio. Vibrio is a very, very nasty little bug that crops up occasionally in our warm coastal waters. While not common, Vibrio is an opportunist, and even the smallest of cuts from a fish hook can open the door to this awful bacteria. Most vulnerable are those who have weak immune systems but anyone can be affected. It is contracted by either eating infected shellfish, or by contact through an open wound on the skin ... such as a stingray wound. Kayak fishing itself can sometimes take a toll on the hands, shins, feet and other parts of the body ... blisters, small nicks and cuts or a scrape with a paddle are common. Wash all cuts with alcohol, a bleach solution or an antibacterial wipe. Hydrogen peroxide can also be effective. The most important thing is to wash the cut or ding thoroughly. If at any time, your injury becomes hot, painful or if you notice swelling or redness that seems out of place for such a small cut or an expanding redness from the site of the injury, seek medical help immediately. Minutes count. If you don't, your whole arm or leg might be lost. No kidding. Vibrio is an anaerobic relative of cholera and lives in warm, brackish waters. Anaerobic means that it does not need oxygen to live or reproduce, so once introduced into a host organism, it multiplies at an astonishing rate and feeds off the host body. That's right ... flesh eating bacteria. There are some experienced guides and fishermen who have suffered through this and it is no joke.

Wind you just can't paddle against. From time to time, you will find yourself in a situation where the wind is against you ... really against you ... and you're not making any headway toward your destination. Always keep your kayak pointed directly into the wind to present the least resistance. Paddling with the wind to your side will expend much more energy than paddling straight into the wind. Even if you have to go a little out of your way, proceed directly into the wind. Keep your paddle low, use as little extra energy as possible as you slowly move your paddle in the water from your foot to behind your shoulders. The slow, steady approach will always eventually assist you to gain headway. Too much splashing and thrashing will simply exhaust you. Lean down, be compact, offer as little frontal area to the wind as possible and you will slowly make headway. As you get close to your destination and with perhaps the advantage of shoreline grasses or a bank to break the wind you will find the paddling easier.

Keep your kayak pointed directly into the wind to present the least resistance

If you are exhausted, try and make your way to an island or duck blind, somewhere that you can climb up on and relax to regain your strength. If there are other boaters in the vicinity, flag someone down and ask them tow your kayak back to your boat or vehicle. It's always better to be on the safe side and ask for help than to spend the night on an island.

Tide that has dropped out ... Kayak fishing on the Texas Coast can be somewhat scientific, at times. If you are not paying attention, tide levels can mean the difference between paddling and walking. And if you are on a "bad" bottom with mud, muck and shell, even walking out may not be possible. Always review tide tables and general water levels in your favorite kayak fishing locations. And remember that even though the tide tables indicate that tide levels are high, weather and fronts may negate those effects and leave you with low water conditions.

When in Doubt, Consult the locals ... they live there!

If you are fishing new areas and are unsure about the tide levels during the times you will be fishing, consult the locals, fishing guides or websites for current information. Summer and Winter Solstice times in late winter and late summer can result in dramatically low water conditions. The day may start out with plenty of water to paddle in, but end up leaving you in the middle of a mile wide shimmering mud flat as the tide drops out in a hurry.

Always be aware of dropping water conditions before you paddle way, way back. If, indeed, you have to walk out instead of paddle as a result of a drop in water levels, make sure that you have the appropriate footwear ... we've talked about this. Tennis shoes, sandals or water socks are simply not sufficient to protect your feet from hidden oyster shells and other sharp objects on the bottom.

Ill health ... You or your fishing buddies. As we've already discussed in some of the other emergency situations, falling ill can be a life or death situation if not handled with swift confidence. Remember, *you* are the only one out there. Help may not be quick to arrive.

If you or your kayak fishing friends becomes ill while out on the water, the first thing to do is to assess the seriousness of the situation. Of course most of us are not doctors, so some situations are beyond our skill levels. But sometimes what appears to be a dire emergency at first, reveals itself to be something more manageable with a cool head and basic first aid.

Good decisions and smart action may mean the difference between life and death for someone with heavy bleeding, heart problems, massive pain or who is unconscious. First, stabilize the situation. Stop the bleeding, and if necessary perform CPR if you know how. Make the person comfortable and set them up for transport and then immediately call 911 on your cell phone. If your cell phone does not work (and it most likely will not), use your waterproof VHF radio to contact the Coast Guard on Channel 16. Tell them your name, the nature of your emergency and your GPS location. Continue to stabilize your situation as best as possible and wait for help. If you decide to transport your friend to a better location and can safely do so, be sure you notify the Coast Guard or the 911 operator of your new location. Time counts in situations such as these. Don't waste it in panic. Keep a cool head and keep everyone informed so that help can reach you as soon as possible.

The Coast Guard monitors VHF Channel 16 at all times

If you are alone and something terrible happens, immediately contact the Coast Guard on your waterproof VHF radio. Give them your name, your emergency and your GPS location and wait for help. Stabilize yourself as best you can. Stay with your kayak. If you have an emergency flag and can reach it, put it up. Use anything that you have that can help the Coast Guard locate a very small you in the vast expanse of reflecting shallow waters. If you can reach your waterproof safety kit, keep your flares or signaling mirror close and use them as help gets close to you. These items when used properly will help the Coast Guard to pinpoint your location.

You're Lost! The Texas Coast is a kayak fishing mecca because of the vastness of the back lakes, marshes and estuary systems that you can paddle and fish. This fact also makes it very easy to get lost, especially if you are paddling areas that are new and unfamiliar.

Being observant helps. Look around ... stand up in your kayak if you have to. When you enter an area, always pick out and locate a couple of landmarks to help you navigate your way back if you do get turned around. Look for things that will stand out ... a tall tree, a distant tower, lighthouse etc. A simple inexpensive compass will show you in which direction you are heading and if you reference it a few times, you'll have a general idea of the direction you should paddle back. A GPS will give you an exact path to backtrack your way out of anywhere that you have paddled, but don't depend solely on the gadget. Understand that the sun rises in the east and sets in the west, so observe where the sun is when you start your trip. Use this information, along with other landmarks that you observed when you started your trip, to gain your bearings if you get lost or turned around. The safest way to make sure you don't get lost is to use your GPS and your compass headings. Both are essential in making sure that you make it back to your launch point. These tools will also help you to develop a sense of the area and identify good fishing and paddling locations for future trips.

If you do get lost ... STOP!! Try to get your bearings if you can by locating those landmarks from the beginning of your trip. Notice where the sun is located in the sky. If you are hot, confused and can't figure out your location or how to backtrack, and you are truly lost, don't hesitate to use your cell phone, VHF radio and GPS. Tell everyone where you went in, how far you think you paddled, what it looks like around you and any other useful information you can give to help someone find you. If you don't have a GPS, use your signal mirror or flares from your emergency kit to let others know where you are. Don't wait all day to make the determination that you are lost. Once the sun goes down, it's definitely a whole other project. And be prepared for a little ribbing when you're found.

Coastal fog can make for an interesting day. Wait for it to burn off if you can. Pay attention to your general surroundings and consult your compass.

You've been hooked! Whoops … The shoe is on the other foot, and you have driven a hook into yourself or your fishing buddy. There are several methods available to remove fish hooks from your body and those of your friends. Did we say "don't panic?" Here are some helpful suggestions.

Hooked in the eye. This is the worst … and another great reason for wearing glasses. Don't try to remove it. Cut the leader or line to relieve all pressure on the hook and place a sterile pad over the eye and the hook together and tape gently in place. Since eyeballs track together, cover the injured persons eyes … both of them, so that the person is not glancing around and causing additional trauma to the injured eye through movement.

Stop Crying … It's no worse than the dentist!!

A. If the hook is fairly deep, try to push it through the skin and clip the barb off. Wash with disinfectant and pull it back out the way it went in.

B. The string pull method allows you to use a piece of fishing line. Press the shank down and pull the hook straight back while whimpering.

C. This method is the quickest … you just yank the sucker out. Press the eye of the hook down and rotate with your pliers so that the exit is pretty much the same as the entrance wound.

An Important Note:
The contents of this book are meant to give the reader an understanding of the subjects of shallow water fishing, weather, safety and potential hazards of being on the water. The author and the publisher make no warranty, expressed or implied, or assume any legal liability or responsibility for the accuracy, completeness, or usefulness of any information contained herein. Always consult professional agencies and medical personnel for accurate information with regard to weather, safety and medical issues.

Chapter 9
Kayak Fishing 101

NOW You're Ready TO FISH!

If you are new to kayak fishing and serious about your future angling success beyond all else then you must realize that it is a journey. There are stunning moments of absolute success and celebration, but the journey can also be an adventure with tedious and frustrating learning curves. Here are a few things that you can do, however, to help you make that trip from bonehead beginner to seasoned angler.

First ... Begin with the right attitude.

No one ever began anything at the top. Everyone and every skill has a beginning point. So be prepared to fail! So what, you're a beginner, you fall, you get stuck in the mud, you hook your shorts with your top water, you forget your sunglasses. You feel like it's the first day of camp and your parents just drove off. Relax ... that's the natural progression of things. Remember, you're in this for the fun of it.

Like anything else, experience matters. No person goes from new kid to old salt in a day. The more you fish, the better it gets!

Sometimes you have to just laugh at yourself! All major successes have been miserable failures at one time or another. That's how we learn. Even the "pros" are still failing and learning - every day - that's what makes them so good. Take the risk to be a great fisherman. The payoff is tremendous! And remember, those seagulls that sound like they're all laughing at you ... probably really are.

Second ... Have realistic expectations. If you were beginning to bowl and you had never even held a bowling ball, you certainly wouldn't expect to bowl a perfect game the first time out. How about during the first month or even the first year of your bowling career? Probably not. It's true that some people get lucky, but you can't bank on luck. The real winner is the person who reviews the game, changes up a bit for next time and makes steady progress toward success.

Be prepared to work at it. It's not easy to be successful. You have to get muddy, wet, tired and frustrated. You have to hold out, hang on, deal with it and make adjustments. Some people call it "paying your dues". Make sure that with each and every fishing experience you log into your knowledge base some fantastic revelation from the day. Every trip adds valuable and unique experiences. Within a short period of time this tenaciousness brings a fisherman out of the beginner's ranks. The angler that has "paid his dues" is no longer just guessing when, where and why the fish are where they are. He or she has actually made mental notes and studied the circumstances of the day and has developed an educated plan built on experience. Catching fish is just part of it. It takes a little time to get there, but after all of that hard work the payoff is pretty darn good.

Bring the Right Stuff

This topic has been fairly well covered in other chapters, but what it really boils down to is paying attention to details before you go kayak fishing. Starting your trip with tennis shoes instead of good wading boots will put you at a disadvantage. Sunglasses that aren't polarized won't give you the ability to see structure, drop-offs, or more importantly, fish. Suncreen and hats are just common sense and will keep you on the water longer. Plenty of water and food are important. Blue jeans and cotton shorts will make for a long, uncomfortable day, so wear quick-dry pants or shorts. Small details can make the big difference between a great day and a frustrating or even painful one.

The Secrets of Sightcasting

Sightcasting is a necessary skill for the shallow water kayak angler. The good news is that "reading the water" is a learned technique. Fishermen new to the sport are often amazed at how guides and seasoned anglers can "see" fish when they can't. By paying attention and with practice, you can teach your eyes to recognize the signs of a fish in the water just as clearly as seeing footprints on a beach.

The Basics

The most essential tool for a beginner sight caster is a good pair of polarized sunglasses. We've already talked about this subject in an earlier chapter. The most popular colors among sight casters are vermillion and amber.

Sunshine and clear water give a beginning sight caster a good, sharp vantage point to start learning the shapes and colors of the different fish under the water. If you are a beginner, you will have more success and will be less frustrated if you start your learning process under optimum conditions. In other words, pick a nice day for your first trip out.

A common sense hint ... get up a little higher if you can. The higher you are above the water, the more and the farther you will be able to see. Go ahead and get out of the boat to wade a shoreline or sand flat. Standing up in your kayak will also give you a better view. The height over the water will make seeing fish easier. Why do you suppose all those wading birds have such long legs?

"Tailing" redfish are often seen solo or in groups. Redfish tend to push through the shallows scaring up baitfish, shrimp and small crabs. Sometimes the entire back may be seen.

Fish Signs

The most obvious sign of fish in shallow water would be when they're feeding in a group with tails up in the air! Or frequently you'll see a big redfish wallowing along a shoreline or in the grass shallows with its back out of the water. A big, heavy push of water that looks like a small boat wake tells you that you've just spooked up a herd of redfish. Obvious signs of fish are easy to recognize ... It's the not-so-obvious signs of fish that the beginning angler will fail to recognize. Here are some basic signs for "what you see, and what it means".

What You See ... Pelicans diving down into the water.
What it Means ... It's likely that redfish or other predators are stirring up the bottom and scattering bait to the surface, giving the pelicans an easy dining opportunity.

What You See ... Rafts of mullet moving quickly and nervously with some of them jumping out of the water.
What it Means ... Predators such as redfish, trout or ladyfish may be in the area keeping the bait moving in a nervous group, sometimes striking from below giving the bait reason to jump.

What You See ... A blue heron standing on a shoreline staring intently at water's edge with an occasional baitfish or shrimp jumping nearby.
What it Means ...There may be a redfish or two feeding along that shoreline, possibly actively pursuing bait there, or laying in wait for the bait to move by. The bird is standing by for the opportunity to feed along with the redfish as they scatter the frantic bait to the surface.

What You See ... Seagulls hovering over shallow water.
What it Means ... Could be a pack of feeding redfish.

What You See ... Seagulls sitting on the water.
What it Means ... Might be feeding redfish present and the gulls are waiting for something stirred from the bottom.

What You See ... Lots of Great White Egrets standing together at the mouth of a lake or bayou.
What it Means ... The current, either tidal or windblown, is moving bait through this area. Where there is moving bait, there are usually feeding predators.

What You See ... A slick on the top of the water.
What it Means ... Feeding redfish in shallow water will emit an oil sheen similar to trout. The sheen is fish oil from digestion and the "crunching up" of bait.

What You See ... Showering bait of any kind.
What it Means ... Predators are feeding on this bait.

What You See ... Large area of mud discoloring the water.
What it Means ... Redfish and or drum stirring up bottom.

What does this wading expert see that you don't?

Mullet or Redfish?

This can be the most agonizing debate an angler will have with when beginning a career as a sight caster. It's no fun spending an afternoon casting to mullet. Water moving in a back lake should never be ignored, but a group of mullet can usually be identified with just a little bit of study. Mullet have forked tails. Mullet are light green or grey, blending into their backgrounds. If you are straining to identify a group of fish moving the water but you can't really see the fish themselves, they are most probably mullet. They are the ghosts in the shallows. Mullet tend to "dart" and move nervously and jittery. They have a good reason to do so ... they spend their entire life on almost every predator's menu!

On the other hand, a redfish has color, be it blue, copper, pink, white or black. Redfish don't move quite so nervously, unless spooked by the angler. They tend to move more like a torpedo through the

Notice Color, Shape and Movement

water. Their tails are flatter and they move with a calm purpose. Groups of mullet create a smaller and more jittery wake on the surface of the water when they move in groups. Redfish create a "bolder", taller wake on the water when they move in groups, especially when they are moving fast! A single redfish moving away from you in the shallow water will create a big v-wake that lasts for a long time and you'll be able to follow the fish's movements swimming away from you for quite a while. A big red will create a mud stir as it launches off into a new direction while a single large mullet scared away will create a smaller v-wake that just disappears with no mud.

Redfish have a distinct shape to their bodies. Their "shoulders" are wide and they look a little like a football. Mullet are slender and their side fins jut outward from their gills.

Most seasoned sight casters will tell you that the thing they notice first when peering into the water looking for a fish, besides the most obvious signs like a group of tails or backs out of the water, would be either movement, shape or color. At first glance, a fish is not as obvious as you might imagine. But, by noticing color, shape or movement that is different from its surroundings, you'll focus on that object until an appropriate identification is made.

When you can see fish with this technique, that's when you know you're starting to "get it"! Develop your instincts and skills of obser-

What you see ... and What it Means?? The key to success in wade fishing is to notice "differences" in the environment. Color, shape and movement are all important factors.

vation using the very basic techniques of color, shape and movement. A seasoned sight caster can scan the surface of the water in a back lake and see a group of redfish by the variations of the surface of the water, the color below it, or just "something different". It's that "something different" that you will want to train yourself to notice. As you do, you will begin to accumulate a vast journal of experiences and knowledge that will continually raise your angling skills to levels that you never thought possible!

Drift

Wade

Fly Fish

Lures &

Bait

Shallow water sight-casting is definitely one of the most exciting techniques an angler can practice. When you know that your hunting skills have improved to the point of seeing and casting to fish accurately, it is extremely satisfying. That's what brings so many good anglers to the sport.

High Probability Fishing Locations

Just as important as all of the obvious signs of fish that you do see, there are a few other details that merit attention when looking for fish. The subject of tides, current, water levels, and wind can be detailed and confusing, but they are all part of the same picture and a basic understanding is helpful.

Tides and water levels are created by moon position, the time of the year and factors such as weather and wind. Major moon phases, such as the full moon and the new moon also contribute to tide velocity and movement.

It is important to realize that significant tides such as the Summer and Winter Solstice times create low water conditions. Spring and Fall "bull tides" bring higher water into the bay systems. Heavy weather systems with strong winds can also push tides in or out. Observing conditions during these dramatic tidal changes can teach a lot about how tides flow during the year. Just as restricting the end of a hose makes the water force stronger, tidal flow is stronger in areas that constrict and direct flow such as jetties, fish passes and major channels. Fishing a structure on a falling tide is a completely different game than fishing the same structure on an incoming tide.

Tidal-Driven Current and Wind-Blown Current

Tides coming in and going out create water current, but so can wind. Since bait moves with the current, and predators feed when bait is moving, understanding windblown current is an important part of understanding where fish may be feeding. Wind can create current when the tides are not moving.

Reading the water for these conditions can make a tough fishing day better! Find the current, you'll find the bait moving and that is where you'll find the fish feeding. Bait doesn't have a choice as to where it goes. Bait is small and is being pushed and pulled by moving currents, either tidal or windblown. Predators, of course, are in the driver's seat and will position themselves in prime bait-moving territory. Most fish feed into a current. Take note of how water is being blown around an island, through a pass, down a slough or through a drain, and you'll be better able to position yourself in a high-probability fishing location where predators are also staging for some food. Become a student of water levels, tidal movements, current and wind and how they impact your favorite fishing places. Having a basic understanding of these conditions will give you an advantage in finding hungry fish!

Styles of Kayak Fishing

Natural Baits or Lure Fishing ... what's the diff? Kayak fishermen typically either lure fish or fly fish. However, a lot of beginners to kayak fishing use bait. If you are a bait fisherman, be prepared to carry a cast net to catch your own live bait. After you catch your bait, you must keep it alive. Some kayak fishermen rig a covered bucket with a battery-powered aerator that rides on top of the kayak. Others simply drag a bait bucket attached to the kayak.

In shallow water, a skillfully worked lure can be just as effective as a live bait.

Kayaks are a perfect fit with shallow water sightcasting.

After a few times of going through the work of finding bait, catching bait, paddling bait around on your kayak and then trying to keep bait alive, you just might decide to try lure fishing. To be honest, because of the compact nature of kayak fishing, it is better suited to lure fishing and fly fishing. That's why most kayak fishermen choose to fish that way. In shallow water, a skillfully worked lure can be just as devastatingly effective as a live bait. Learning the techniques of fishing different types of lures and making them appear appealing and realistic to predators just takes practice.

So Why Fly Fish? It's just a matter of time before a lure fisherman in a kayak will give fly fishing some serious thought. All too often, even with a good presentation, that big top water lure will splash down like a returning space capsule and spook the fish. Shallow water requires a softer touch. Fly fishing, by virtue of its quiet presentation of the fly, the ease of repositioning the cast and the natural look of the fly is a perfect fit with shallow water sightcasting. Gently placing a fly between two hungry redfish cruising the shallows water is not only fun, it's often more productive than trying to get them to chase that top water after they've run from it.

Should I fish from the kayak or get out and wade? Do both. The benefits of getting out of your kayak and wading to fish can be easily seen. Sitting down on top of your kayak, you are a little more than alligator eye level with the water. Wade fishing offers more height and a much better vantage point for sightcasting. By getting out of the kayak, a wade fisherman will not only be able to see bottom structure and habitat close by, but will also have a "big picture" view of tide and wind influences.

If the wind is blowing, wade fishing can give an angler the benefit of really slowing down the fishing. A kayak in windy conditions can cover a flat very quickly and a fisherman sitting in a fast drifting kayak can miss a lot of important signs. Getting out of the kayak to wade allows an angler to slowly work the grass edges, potholes and guts. Wading allows fishermen to study and read the water.

On the other hand, drifting in your kayak is by far the stealthiest way to fish. Wading is by nature noisy even for those skilled and stealthy waders. And getting in and out of your kayak can be a little unwieldy, especially for beginners, not to mention make a lot of noise. Paddles, rods, reels, and discovering that you've been sitting on a sandwich all afternoon can all add to the start of a noisy dismount! Then you'll have to figure out how not to dump the stuff out of your tank well as you "gracefully" swing your legs and stingray boots out of the kayak and slip into the water. Sometimes just staying in your kayak and planning a quiet approach to your fish is more efficient.

Kayak fishermen who stay in their kayak to fish need a good understanding of how their kayak drifts in the wind. Setting up a drift over a prime fishing area usually requires a drift anchor to slow down and sometimes to direct your drift. Most kayak fishermen who prefer to stay in their kayak while fishing almost always have an adjustable drift anchor system mounted along one side of the kayak. With a rope, a clip and a pulley, kayak drift anglers can quickly adjust the angle of their drift with a pull of the rope.

Rudders are a favorite of die hard drift anglers. By utilizing foot pegs connected to a rudder system the fisherman has hands-free drift positioning. If this is your primary style of kayak fishing, a rudder is an invaluable tool.

Go ahead ... Stand up! Remember the discussion and benefits of having height on the water? Standing up on your kayak if you've got a kayak that can be stood upon ... and there are a few on the market... offers the most height you can have while fishing! Extra height will provide lots of extra visibility, not just in the water right around you, but a better "big picture" view of your fishing area as well. Some anglers who fish standing up prefer to keep their rods in a holder around their waist.

Most anglers who fish this way will use their paddles like a push pole to move their kayak through the water. But this presents the

Standing up on your kayak gives a commanding view perfect for the serious sight caster.

problem of where to set the paddle down when fish are sighted and you are ready to cast. Setting the paddle on the kayak can cause noise and it will almost certainly be in the way. The solution is to have the paddle on a leash. This allows the angler to quietly set the paddle in the water rather than clonking it on the boat before picking up their rod and reel or fly rod to cast. Setting the paddle in the water tethered with a leash allows the angler to quietly deal with embarrassing "paddle noise syndrome". Also, if you aren't concerned about your paddle, you won't have to take your eyes off the fish while you bend down to pick up your rod. Now, of course, once that fish is hooked and fighting, you would do well to remember that paddle on the leash in the water! Besides putting your paddle on a leash, another tip is keeping a clean cockpit, particularly important for fly casters. Fly casters require a clean kayak cockpit for stripping

Positioning ...

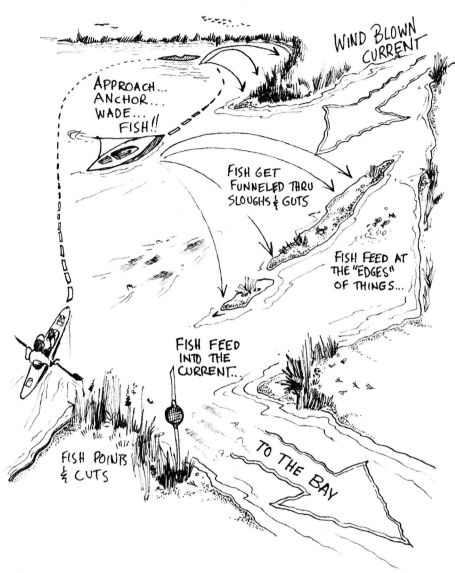

Positioning your kayak means considering wind direction and velocity, tidal flow, the current direction, your paddling skills and your casting skills ...

All in order to position your kayak to best cast to the fish.

line into. Rod holders, foot pegs and other devices mounted in and around the cockpit area will surely attract and tangle fly line and that's when the fun begins! Fighting a fish standing up in your kayak can make for quite an adventure!

About Positioning ...

This can be one of the most important techniques for kayak fishermen to master. Positioning your kayak means considering wind direction and velocity, tidal flow, current direction, your paddling skills and your casting skills ... All in order to position your kayak to cast to the fish. Where will the wind take you and your boat ... and how can you put yourself in the most optimum spot to take advantage of it? You will want to visualize not only where your kayak will be, but in what direction you will be casting. Couple this with the fact that the fish are usually moving as well and it becomes clear that positioning can be as important as finding the fish in the first place! Putting your kayak upwind of your fish, perhaps setting an anchor and then understanding how wind direction will swing the bow or stern of the kayak will enable you to be in the right position to cast accurately to the target. Thinking in advance and using your experience on the water will give you a better understanding of "positioning". If your kayak is consistently out of position, you will have little success with casting and always be frustrated.

Positioning a kayak properly in a variety of fishing situations takes practise but is well worth it.

67

Forget the Orange Roughy or Tilapia ... this is fresh seafood at its best!

Fish as Food

Decided to keep a few fish for dinner ... Great! Now what? Dragging them behind the kayak all day on a stringer isn't a very good idea, especially when the water is hot in the summer. Fish won't live that long under those conditions. Some people might use one of those "donuts" that have the floating ring, but it's still a "drag". A dedicated fish bag, which can be as simple as an extra soft-sided cooler is a much better solution. Store it in the interior hatch of your kayak, or across the bow or stern, if you don't have an interior storage location. There are fish holding bags specifically for kayakers on the market but a soft-sided cooler can be a lot cheaper and work just as well. Fill this extra cooler with ice and you'll have the perfect place to keep your fish fresh and good until you get back to your boat or truck.

Kayak Courtesy

Fishing courtesy in general sometimes seems like a lost art. There are so many boats on the water and so many fishermen all competing for the same resource. There is only one real rule of fishing courtesy ... "treat people the way you want to be treated". It really is that simple. Non-courteous angling behavior includes: Cutting through another angler's drift, be they in a powerboat or a kayak; Jumping ahead or cutting off another angler wadefishing or kayaking a shoreline; Fishing too closely to another kayaker or powerboater.

Those are just a few. Whether by ignorance of the spoken or unspoken rules of outdoor sportsmanship, or by a blatant action, bad behavior can turn a good fishing day bad. If somebody is in your favorite spot, move on. They were there first. Keep it light, pay attention and stop and think before you proceed in areas where others are fishing. We're all out there for the fun of it.

Courtesy is Contagious ... Always use at least two fingers when waving to airboat operators. They are the only ones who might possibly be able to get to you in a real pinch.

Kayak Fishing ... A "Perfect" Way to Fish

Now that you are armed with most of the important information and aspects a kayak angler needs to be successful in the saltwater, you are ready for a fish-packed season of "catching"!

The main reason that kayak fishing has taken over on the Texas Coast is that it is nearly a "perfect" way to fish! Silent, stealthy and effective, anglers can become part of the natural scene rather than a noisy intrusion. In a kayak, you are able to slide through the lakes and marshes observing details that other anglers miss. The kayak angler becomes one of the smartest predators in the shallows, intimately interacting with the surface of the water, the feeding birds and the movements of bait and fish.

Get your kayak in the water ... Fish as much as possible. Utilizing the tools and information in this book, your kayak angling skills will improve, and with time on the water, you'll have an unfair advantage over other fishermen! The peace, solitude and beauty of the Texas Coast with its vast saltwater lakes and marshes is a rare gift. Kayaks give the angler a relaxing and enjoyable opportunity to spend time with friends and family ... and a great fish dinner as well!

About conservation: As you evolve as an angler on the Texas Coast, you will see first hand the importance of conservation and protection of the environment in which we paddle, boat and wade. Keeping our shorelines clean and our sea grasses protected is more important than ever. Preserving and passing on the beauty and bounty of the wild Texas Coast is the ultimate legacy for the future enjoyment of this fantastic resource. Paddle on! ... But leave nothing behind but your warm memories.

Capt. Sally

Captain Sally's Basic Tackle List

Fly Fishing Equipment

Fly Rods & Reels: 9' 6-9 weight, medium fast/fast action fly rods. Quality fly reel with smooth drag and 100+ yards of 20lb Dacron backing.

Line: Weight forward floating fly line designed for salt water and warm temperatures.

Fly Line Tapers: Saltwater tapers, clouser tapers or redfish tapers

Line Cleaners & Treatments

Leaders / Tippets: 10-15 lb. 9' tapered leaders, either knotless or hand-tied, furled or braided 10-16 lb tippet

Fly Selections:· Shrimp, baitfish, crab patterns all work well in sizes #4 or #6. Clouser minnows in white/chartreuse, white/pink, white/olive, white/natural in #4 or #6. Spoon flies in gold, plum, peach in size #4 or #6 Popper flies in white/chartreuse, gold, white/red. Sea Ducers in natural, chartreuse/white, pink/white, natural in #2 or #4

Conventional Tackle

Rods and Reels: 7' medium/fast to fast action spinning rod in medium light. Matching reel with 10-12 lb test line

Tackle and Lures: Weedless Gold Spoons 1/8 and 1/4 ounce.

Topwater Lures: Smaller-sized topwaters lures in light colors, such as bone/silver, bone/chartreuse, baby redfish and baby trout colors. Dark colors include, black/chartreuse, black/red, gold/black and baby redfish.

Soft Plastics: Paddle-tailed casting plastics in light colors, such as pumpkin seed/chartreuse, pearl (or glow) chartreuse, and dark colors such as black/chartreuse, plum/chartreuse, motor oil, avocado, firetiger.

Jig Heads: 1/16, 1/8 and 1/4 ounce sizes.

Basics: The general rule of thumb with regard to lure color is that light colored lures can be used when the water color is clear to good, and on sunny days. Darker colors should be used when water color is off, or when fishing a cloudy or windy day.

Fly fishing enthusiasts generally wind up tying, and trying, various designs of their own.

Kayak Fishing Checklist:

Use this checklist each time you go out.

- ☐ Fishing license
- ☐ Kayak Safety Kit
- ☐ Hat with dark under brim
- ☐ Polarized Sunglasses / Lense Cleaners
- ☐ Line Clippers / Pliers / Hook-Out / Hemostats
- ☐ Paddle, spare paddle / Paddle Leash
- ☐ Cell phone / GPS / VHF radio ... and some batteries
- ☐ Waterproof bags for above
- ☐ Waterproof camera / Binoculars
- ☐ Aerial Map or Chart / Compass
- ☐ Rods, Reels & Rod Leash
- ☐ Tackle Bag / Wading Belt
- ☐ Soft-sided cooler with water
- ☐ Extra soft sided cooler and ice for fish

Continued on the next page ...

- [ ] Wading Boots ... No tennis shoes, sandals or water shoes.
- [ ] Microfiber Socks or ski-boot liners for wading boots
- [ ] Light, quick-dry clothing, not jeans or heavy cotton
- [ ] Rain jacket or windbreaker
- [ ] Lunch in waterproof zip-lock bags ... Bring plenty!
- [ ] Sunscreen / Lip Balm
- [ ] Other stuff ... but not too much!!

_____

_____

_____

_____

_____

_____

_____

_____

About the Author:

Sally Ann Moffett has been a lifelong lover of the outdoors and grew up along the shores of Lake Erie. Her father was a boating and fishing enthusiast and the family spent many summers aboard their Chris Craft cabin cruiser fishing, camping and exploring along the inlets and bays. He shared with her his fishing and boating knowledge and often joked that Sally was the son he'd never had!

She obtained her 25 ton Near Coastal Masters United States Coast Guard Captain's license and started her own fishing guide business in 1998. She has gained wide recognition as the very first professional kayak fishing guide on the Texas coast, as well as the first female fly fishing guide there as well. She has been featured on several television shows, and in national and regional magazines, and contributes articles to many magazines as well. She is a founding member of the Texas Woman Fly Fishers Club, and an advisory director of the Texas Lady Anglers. Captain Sally is a regular voice on several urban radio shows and is also a member of the Coastal Conservation Association, Saltwater Conservation Association and Ducks Unlimited.

Above all, Captain Sally loves fishing the wild coast of Texas with its birds, wildlife and unique and pristine marine environment… and sharing it with her clients and friends.

www.CaptainSally.com

Order additional copies of this book by visiting
www.SaltGrassPress.com

Coming soon ...

Kayak Fishing the Mid-Texas Coast

The Kayaker's Guide to fishing spots, launching
areas, bays and flats around the mid-coast area,
including information on the extensive
Lighthouse Lakes Trails and other kayak areas.

The Kayak Fisherman's Log Book

A personal log book ready for notes on temperature,
tides, fish caught and other important details.
Invaluable for the serious fisherman.